Pigs ina Poke™
Collection #1

Pigs ina Poke™

Collection #1

D. A. Hammond

with satirical prose by
Lawrence K. DeLamarter and Bradley Marion

Beech River Books
Center Ossipee, N.H.

BℝB
Beech River Books
P.O. Box 62, Center Ossipee, N.H. 03814
1-603-539-3537
www.beechriverbooks.com

First edition

Library of Congress Cataloging-in-Publication Data

Hammond, D. A. (Duane A.)
Pigs ina poke, collection #1 / D.A. Hammond ;
with satirical prose by Lawrence K. DeLamarter and Bradley Marion.
p. cm.
ISBN 0-9776514-6-0 (pbk.)
1. Hammond, D. A. (Duane A.) 2. Swine in art. 3. Swine--Humor. 4. Puns and punning.
I. DeLamarter, Lawrence K. II. Marion, Bradley. III. Title.
IV. Title: Pigs in a poke, collection #1. V. Title: Pigs ina poke, collection no. 1.

NC139.H255A4 2006
741.5'6973--dc22
2006028214

ISBN-13: 978-0-9776514-6-7 (pbk.)

Printed in China

Dedication

To my wife, Sandy, who picks up my dirty socks, chases after me
with a dustpan, introduced me to a bar of soap and made many of
the suggestions that helped me produce this art and this book,
instead of just a bunch of garbage.

Table of Contents

2007: The Year of the Pig

Foreword

This book is a porcine masterpiece. I couldn't put it down. Then again, I just looked at the pictures. The unkosher style of Hammond is most refreshing.

Not since Mommy read me the *Three Little Pigs*, have I been so moved by a story book. Every pigophile in America must have a copy of this charming book.

I suggest you go out and buy copies for all your friends. (They told me to say this.)

I hope they give me a free copy for writing this. I also hope that the movie version comes out, before this book is published. I'm actually more of a movie critic. I ain't never been no good at reading.

—D. Arthur Schaefer

Introduction

As late as 2002, I was working primarily in watercolors and working on a variety of subjects: seascapes, landscapes, cityscapes, portraits. I came across a box of pastel pencils that I had had for years, perhaps since the time I had attended the Museum School of Fine Arts in Boston. Both my wife, Sandy, and I had graduated from that school, (she with honors), and as I began working in this medium again I found that I loved the detail and intense color one could achieve. I was working very hard—in 2002/2003 I produced over three hundred works per year. Then one day, in a moment of deswine inspiration, I produced my first painting of a pig.

People seemed to love the pig right away, but for me it raised a real problem because I couldn't think of a title. I thought and thought and eventually I came up with ORKYPAY, which is pig-Latin for Porky. I liked the name and I resolved, then and there, that I would never do another pig painting without already having a title in mind. The result was that night I didn't get any sleep; neither did Sandy, because I kept waking her up to tell her of the next humorous title and image. I wrote down twenty-five titles that night, and ever since, I keep having ideas for new works faster than I can render them.

The idea, of course, always revolves around some *double entendre*, parody, or situation made funny by replacing a human with a pig. I try to bring the work to a level of art that distinguishes it from a cartoon. Art should evoke a response from the viewer. As we walk through a gallery or exhibit, we are moved by the subject, color and rendition of the work and might feel awed, uplifted, anguished or shamed by what we observe. I hope the art world can also accept humor and that you are moved to chuckle and laugh as you page through this book. Maybe you'll think of a new title yourself that you can share with me. Please write *dah@pigsinapoke.com*.

Section 1

Pigs and Fine Art

The Squeal

For centuries art was pre-occupied with religious or heroic themes, or pieces obviously intended to win patronage from the wealthy and powerful. With the rise of a middle-class that looked at art as something more personal to interact with, painters began to portray more sentimental and humanistic scenes. The art scene was revolutionized by the arrival of impressionism when artists began for the first time to freely mix some of their own feelings into their technique, and Parisian artists' highly personalized styles became as much a part of the work as the subject.

"The Squeal" is one of the hallmarks of the next big movement, when the artist invited the viewer to join him in an emotional response. *Expressionism* was a rejection of the excessive intellectualism that characterized the French art scene, embracing raw, "gut" feeling as a universal language that speaks across cultures, perhaps even across species. The viewer, especially males, can hardly help but empathize with the instinctual reaction of the poor pig in the foreground who has just received a wedgie from the guy with the cane. The swirling red sky has been much remarked on by critics as an icon for our deepest fears and innermost torment.

The Squeal

Pigasso

The most famous artist of modern times was strongly influenced in his earlier years by his exposure to the works of the Fauvists, (a term, derived from the French word for "wild beasts," that was used by Parisian critics to describe a group of artists whose work at one exhibit included many unusual portrayals of animals). Pigasso's prolific work is often divided into periods, the Pink Period being characterized by less hairy flesh tones than those he favored during his Boar-ing Period.

The anguish felt by this sensitive artist upon his first viewing of small cubes of ham served on platters with toothpicks led to his revolutionary Cubist works. He threw toothpicks over his paintings and then painstakingly traced the resulting angles, later working them into his figures or filling in the spaces between his "cubes" with dark shadows. He went further as his work matured. He cut out the sketches along the random lines created by his scattered toothpicks, then threw all the pieces up in the air, half of which often blew away through a window in his studio. The rest he reassembled as an "Abstraction," meaning that he made a loose attempt to put them back somewhere near where they might have been in the original, though not necessarily, depending on his mood and how much alcohol he might have consumed.

Pigasso

Onamay Isalay

Historians have long struggled to solve the secret code Da Vinci used to record his most important discoveries. He encrypted the words so cleverly that for centuries his fascinating discoveries remained a mystery. It was also rumored that some of his most famous masterpieces had been painted over works that could give clues to enigmatic and esoteric sources that may have motivated his genius.

New, sophisticated computer-aided imaging techniques, (originally developed by NASA to see through the thick clouds encircling the planet Venus), have allowed us to look through the surface layers of Leonardo's art and see the incredible designs that have been hidden there for centuries. The one on the "Mona Lisa" canvas is particularly remarkable. Not only does it raise new questions about what qualities Da Vinci was attempting to capture, (sending leading art historians back to do more careful studies of the famous snout and giving new insights into the spacing of the eyes) but it may also be a Rosetta's stone, unlocking Leonardo's curious back-hand writing. In small, barely readable letters hidden on the extreme edge of the canvas under the artist's signature we can clearly read: "First sound becomes last, followed by —*ay*," a system the famous Florentine referred to as "pig Latin."

Onamay Isalay

American Hogothic

Iowa has long been seen as the capital of American Hog culture. The density of the swine population is only rivaled by Denmark and Poland and it is the place where the next fad first appears. "Everything starts on the coasts—L.A., Frisco, Seattle and D.C., the Big Apple, and Boston—when you look at the big trends in human culture. But it's Cedar Rapids, Des Moines, and Ames when you're talking about the latest *sowcial* trends," says Harry Razorback of the Conservatory of Art. "This is where the urbanization of ham really caught on and it was in the larger congregations of pork bellies that progressive and populist ideas took hold."

The University of Iowa at Ames had offered Agricultural degrees in swineherding since its opening years but only recently recognized the potential of offering degrees in Swine Education. In only a few generations, the educated classes of pigs demanded instructors from their own species and soon after pigs began entering other fields of post-secondary concentration as well.

The noted painting, "American Hogothic" by Grunt Woodham, is a tribute to the rising status of pigs in the arts as well as on the farm. It caused a stir when it was first exhibited at the Art Institute of Chicago and was awarded a $300 prize. The highly detailed style and rigid arrangement of figures were inspired by Northern Renaissance art, which the artist studied during three trips to Europe. It has become one of the more famous and widely recognized paintings and is a primary example of Regionalism, a movement that aggressively opposes European abstract art. Some believe that the artist intentionally chose to make his male figure as boaring as possible, but Woodham denies this and states that he meant to represent him as serious, tidy, flexible and responsible—the opposite of those derogatory epitaphs he despises: "a happy, go-lucky piggy, a filthy pig, pig-headed, or pigging out."

American Hogothic

Vincent van Hogh

This artist is known as a tragic figure, alleged to have cut off part of his own ear in a fit of madness, brought on by depression, absinthe, and hypersensitivity. However, some controversy continues to swirl around the subject of his bandaged ear and the extent of his mania and injury. In my own examination of some rare copies of letters he wrote to his brother, Theehogh, Vincent mentions that he painted his famous "Starry Night" by gazing at the image of the night sky as reflected in a fogged up mirror.

"The effect was both Brilliant and Diffuse, but as I found it necessary to continually breathe on the mirror to maintain its fogginess, I gradually entered a State induced by hyperventilation where I Felt unsteady on my feet and the sky was Swirling above," Vincent writes and these lines are commonly quoted. But what follows a little later in the same letter often fails to be mentioned.

"As the Fog dissipated and I was once more induced to apply the Remedy, I couldn't help but notice the Ugliness of my right ear against the Overwhelming Beauty of the Beyond. I applied bandages, Theehogh, and took other remedies."

The bandaged ear also appears in a self-portrait, but Van Hogh may have been alluding to the ear tag he wore, its reflection perhaps or image troubling him in a moment otherwise transcendent, or perhaps reminding him of the expression "in a pig's ear" meaning that things might come out badly. He was determined at this time to look at things as optimistically as possible and to avoid negativity, so he either bandaged his ear to hide the tag or perhaps removed the tag and applied bandages in an effort to make his ear lie back against his head more attractively, (the tag would have made it flop forward). He did have an interest in a local sow among the peasants, it is said, who may have spurned his advances at first.

Vincent van Hogh

Le Pigmy Lautrec

Although his short stature made him look like a side-show freak, Hamri "le pigmy" was an active and debonair gentleham and his artwork captured the Pigarisian nightlife of the period. He was born of a prominent lineage and could trace his lineage back for a thousand years. Hamri's sire was rich, handsome and eccentric, but Hamri was weak and often sick. An abnormality left him with laughably small and weak ham muscles, so he decided to live wholly for his art.

He styed in the Montmarte section of Pigaris and indulged in a bohamian life style. Instead of sticking his snout high in the air like other boarish aristocrats, he rolled in the filth of the cabarets and recorded his observations in colorful posters that made pigpens such as the Moulin Rouge overnight sensations. He reached the height (no pun intended) of his short career in the 1890s, "la belle épigque," and knew many of the other famous painters who lived and worked in Pigaris at the same time. They included Pigas, Sowzanne, Gaugham, Van Hogh, Sowrat, and Pignoir. His *joink de vivre* was celebrated a bit too much, and the effect of hogskins of absinthe broke down his health, but after his death, his paintings and posters have been in great demand and bring high prices at auctions and art sales.

Le Pigmy Lautrec

Andy Warthog

It all flowed from one central insight: in a culture glutted with information, where most things are experienced second hand through television, there is a role for affectless art. Or, as Andy once put it, "If the sponsors of soap operas don't have to apologize for repeating the same commercials all day long, I shouldn't have to explain a soup can."

Warthog embodied that American view of celebrity—the famous image of a pig, the famous brand name—had become icons, taking the place of both the sacred and the solid. Marilham has replaced the Virgin of Medieval art. The attempt of artists to capture the subtleties of light and color have been thrown aside for the pigheaded realism of the mass advertised product.

This fascination yet indifference to the object mimics the way we are invited to line up at the feed trough as a consumer society and pig-out on bland reproductions of what we've tasted many times before. Warthog puts his hoof in it when he says "I have a taste for the boaring."

He's perhaps more famous for having said "In the future everyone will be pork chops for fifteen minutes." Some have taken this as a visionary statement anticipating today's microwave culture or simply as the condensation of PLOP culture to a single phrase. Image overload has brought us to the condition that we've become uninvolved in trying to make sense of it anyway.

Andy Warthog

Vitruvian Ham

An amazing preservation! One of Leonardo da Vinci's famous notebooks has recently resurfaced. It is well-known that the famous artist and inventor kept hundreds of journals, but only a few have survived into the modern era. Construction of a pet supplies store in southern France was interrupted for several weeks when a plasterer discovered some unusual artifacts behind a brick wall that was being torn out as part of the renovation. Experts rushed to the scene, and although not yet fully-accepted by the scientific community as authentic, more than one prominent pedagogue has already asserted that their studies of the work, the materials and linguistics all would coincide with a date of the early 1500s and a Florentine origin.

The drawings seem to pre-date some of Da Vinci's famous anatomical studies and suggest that, before he had access to morgues and human cadavers, he had engaged in an intense study of porcine proportionality. The young Leonardo would have had easy access to butchered animals among the Italian peasantry and wrote excitedly of what he referred to as "the law of thirds" based upon the spacing from the eyebrows to the top of the forehead, the identical length being also found in measuring from the eyes to the tip of the snout, and again from the nostrils to the hairs of the chinny-chin-chin. The symmetry and proportion Leonardo discovered in this work would later be reinforced by his studies of the human form. Certain experts assert that the Master may have used underpaintings of pigs to establish "the divine proportions" he used in his famous portraits, finding the pigs to be more cooperative models.

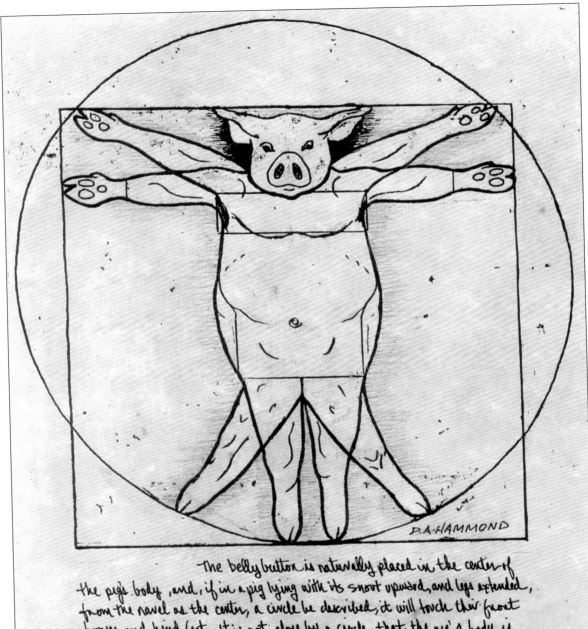

The belly button is naturally placed in the center of the pig's body, and, if in a pig lying with its snout upward, and legs extended, from the navel as the center, a circle be described, it will touch their front hooves and hind feet. It is not alone by a circle, that the pig's body is thus circumscribed, as may be seen by placing it within a square. For measuring from the pig's feet to the snout, and then across the legs fully extended, we find the latter measure equal to the former.

Vitruvian Ham

Pigs Play Porker

Thursday nights the gals get out to "Yoga for Fitness" class, so the guys have a chance to do a little workout of our own. Harry got one of those new-fangled exercise machines that come with a set of instructions in twelve languages—turned out they were all Greek to me. We were supposed to set it up in Harry's basement, but we never could get the darn thing together. Called a few of the boys to try to get some technical help, and while we were studying the manual, we thought we might as well play a few hands and enjoy a brewski or two.

Harry won quite a pot that night, which eased some of the pain he might have felt about not getting the machine together. Of course, we all agreed to come back next Thursday and have another go at it. Harry says he might see if they've got some kind of video explaining how the thing goes together, but a year's gone by and he hasn't gotten a reply yet from the manufacturer. He don't seem too anxious 'bout it, though.

Pigs Play Porker

The Two Piglets

Two cherubs rest at the foot of the painting of the "Pigstine Madonna," by Italian Renaissance painter Raphael. They're looking up, but do not appear to be contemplating the saints or the opening in the heavens. They're leaning on the balustrade as if they've been enjoying a conversation, but the words have led to sighs and a reverie.

Critics have insisted that Raphael intended to suggest that the *amorini* are thinking about love, but he has rendered them as such chubby creatures that it is hard to imagine that their tiny wings could generate enough lift to launch all that body weight.

"Cherry pie," begins the first of the *putti*.

"Banana split: three scoops, piles of whipped cream, topped with a maraschino," replies the other.

"Black cherries over Black Forest cake with almond ice cream," suggests the older *putti*.

"Pound cake soaked in maple syrup and topped with candied cherries," the younger one continues.

"God created so many healthy ways to enjoy cherries," they sigh together.

The Two Piglets

The Birth of Pigus

Boticelli's canvas that hangs today in the Uffizi in Florence was painted for a mass audience. The original work, however, remained hidden in the villa of Lorenzo de' Medici for 520 years until its recent rediscovery.

The Medici were famous for their patronage of art and even more famous for their international banking system and political scheming, but the family's roots were old and they had once been swineherds in the fields of Lombardy along the banks of the river Arno. Lorenzo was a notorious cynic as well as a corrupt despot and wanted a painting of the birth of the goddess of love with earthy, rather than heavenly, allusions.

Boticelli apparently complied. While retaining some of the important elements of the myth, such as the birth from water, he manages to weave in subtle indications of love's other aspects in both the countenance of the goddess and the suggestion of garbage in the background. The picture forms such a harmonious pattern, the figure depicted with such graceful movements and melodious lines that we fail to notice the unusually thin neck or the way the left arm is attached to the body. Instead we carry away the impression of an infinitely tender and corpulent being, wafted to our shores as a gift from heaven.

The Birth of Pigus

The Creation of Ham

While cleaning the ceiling of the Pigstine Chapel, technicians brought back to life the vivid color and incredible passion rendered by the famous artist.

One cannot but hear a hundred bows with stretched pig sinew suddenly pulled together, the continuo melting into triumphant blasts of Renaissance horns, and then the sonorous voice of the narrator drifts over the music, with these familiar phrases from Willham Shakespeare...

[HAMLET]   What a piece of work is a ham!
How noble in reason!
how infinite in faculties!
in form and moving,
how express and admirable!
in action how like an angel!
in apprehension, how like a god!
the beauty of the world!
the paragon of animals!

The Creation of Ham

Section 2

Pigs, Literature, Science and Music

Ludpig van Beethoven's Fifth

Viennese devotees of new music made their way to the Weiner Theater for a premiere of Beethoven's symphony. The theater had no heat and the orchestra struggled through some poorly rehearsed parts of the four hour program rather painfully. The whole experience led one listener to comment later that "one can have too much of a good thing—and still more of a loud [performance]."

Music critics had little to say about the Fifth at its premiere. However, a year and a half later, the Allgeswine musicalische Stytung gave a highly favorable review of another performance. The reviewer, E. T. A. Hoghmann, described the work this way: "Radiant shots pierce the deep night and we become aware of clinking ice cubes which, rocking back and forth, close in on us and destroy all within us except the pain of endless longing."

The reviewer may have been excessively sentimental, but the musical meaning of the opening notes is clearly Beethoven's attempt to snort out the key of his symphony. He then repeats the rhythm throughout the work. Sometimes faint, distant oinks, sometimes triumphant bellows, the four-note pattern becomes the recurring hoof print that unites the symphony's movements.

Ludpig van Beethoven's Fifth

AKA William Shakespeare

Indeed, there has been much scholarly speculation about William Shakespeare, known in pig circles as "The Immortal Lard." Just who was this genius? Did he actually write the many plays and sonnets which bear his name?

Recent research has revealed that Shakespeare actually did write Shakespeare! From HAMLET to JULIUS SAUSAGE to TWO GENTLEMEN OF BOLOGNA every single line can be attributed to Shakespeare.

Here's a little quiz to test your own Shakespearean knowledge. (Write the name of the play after the quote.)

1. "A pig! a pig! my kingdom for a pig!"

   _____

2. "What's in a name? That which we call a pork chop
   By any other name would smell as sweet."

   _____

3. "The pig's skin lives after him.
   The flesh is oft ground up with his bones."

   _____

4. "Alas, poor Porick! I knew him, Horatio."

   _____

Answers: 1. King Richlard III 2. Porkeo & Juliet 3. Julius Sausage 4. Hamlet

A.K.A. William Shakespeare

Sir Oinksalot

When it comes to acts of piggery, there was never a knight quite like Sir Oinksalot.

In the countryside of Merrie Olde England, they still sing this bold French knight's praises in the following ballad.

Sir Oinksalot

Who can pull your sausages from
A roaring fire?
Sir Oinksalot. Oink-oink-oinksalot.

Who can save a maiden sow
From straits most dire?
Sir Oinksalot. Oink-oink-oinksalot.

Who's the most gallant knight
You've ever met?
Sir Oinksalot. Oink-oink-oinksalot.

Whose pork-filled lance
Is en brochette?
Sir Oinksalot. Oink-oink-oinksalot.

From blood pudding to pork pâté,
He's a one pig charcuterie.

Sir Oinksalot

Ernest Hamingway

"In the summer of that year, we lived in a pigsty on a farm that looked across a gully. In the mud in that sty were scraps of garbage, rotten and delicious in the sun."

The opening lines of Ernest Hamingway's novel, A FAREWELL TO ARMS AND SHOULDERS AND BUTTS, ring as clean and pure as when he first penned them.

No writer had more impact on writers and writing of the twentieth century. Hamingway's style is as elegant and thin as a slice of prosciutto. His great novels like THE PORK PIE ALSO RISES and FOR WHOM THE SALAMI TOLLS have become immortal classics.

Ernest Hamingway

Truham Capote

A simple Southern pig, Truham was catapulted to early fame by his great novel, BREAKFAST AT DENNY'S. This is a charming portrayal of a young sow, Holly Gonotsolightly, and her passion for large breakfasts. Who can forget Holly's first encounter with a Denny's Grand Slam Breakfast? Or her ordering "sides" of ham with red gravy and link sausages with the Big Skillet Special.

His next great book took a more sinister bent. IN COLD MUD was a gruesome account of a Mid-Western pigsty.

With his large horn rimmed glasses and his signature high-pitched squeal, Truham remains a literary icon.

Truham Capote at Sardi's

Ham String Quartet

Acclaim

"... with musicians like this there must be some hope for humanity."

— *Swine Times* (London)

"The performances were everything we have come to expect from this superb ensemble: technically resourceful, musically insightful, rich food breaks and always interesting."

— *The New York Swines*

"Few swine quartets have regularly displayed such individuality among members of the same sty—an ideal stance for coloring and differentiating the complex strands of the fugues."

— *The Philhogdelphia Inquirer*

"The precision and grace with which the ensemble dispatched the opening of the final movement was breathtaking, and the way they attacked their snacks was equally impressive."

— Hamdante.com

"The group has staked its claim to being indispensable hams in a world that is constantly devouring even the most excellent ensembles."

— *Pigsday*

"These are high-powered performances with at times terrifying attack and explosive accenting . . . they are mightily impressive and each weighs in at over 400 pounds."

— *Gramhogphone*

"The Ham String Quartet . . . has the easy virtuosity, precise sense of ensemble, rhythmic vigor and a maple-cured, smoky flavor . . ."

— *The Washington Fencepost*

"The Ham String performances represented an extraordinary fusion of experience and authority with audacity and freshness. Nothing boaring about this performance!"

— *The Hogston Globe*

Ham String Quartet

Sir Francis Bacon

Sir Francis Bacon, once thought to have written Shakespeare*, was a brilliant literary figure in his own right. Sir Francis was born in Hampshire into an ancient family of hogs. As a piglet he attended Eatin' and went on to Pig's College at Hogsford University.

After the obligatory tour of The Continent, where he visited Bologna, Vienna, Frankfort and Hamburg, he returned to England. Sir Francis served both at court and in Parliament. He retired from politics early, because of a scandal over pork barrel legislation.

Bacon spent the rest of his life writing and lived to a ripe old age which he attributed to the simple fact, "I never smoked."

*A scholarly study in this very book maintains that, amazingly, Shakespeare actually wrote Shakespeare.

Sir Francis Bacon

Albert Swinestein

"Mathematics are well and good but nature keeps dragging us around by the nose."

In spite of his great fame as one of the most eminent thinkers of his time, Albert Swinestein was prone to making statements of simple common sense. He often alluded to his disdain for the type of education that drills old ideas into young brains instead of encouraging their brains to soar in the lofty spaces of imagination. He said, regarding his life's work, "Since the mathematicians have invaded the theory of relativity, I do not understand it myself anymore."

One of Swinestein's favorite anecdotes was about how he came up with the simplified equation $E=mc^2$. "I was rather hungry at the time and couldn't stop thinking about bagels. Of course, that led me to think about cream cheese, (c^2), which wasn't a very deep or original idea, but then I began to explore the relationship of the area of the hole to the area of the whole. This required the consumption (Eating = E) of more (m) bagels than I'd like to admit, but I was eventually satisfied. 'Eureka!' I exclaimed, 'The world needs one equation that can explain the whole universe.' "

Great advice from a true genius: "If you're trying to develop a good idea, chew on it awhile."

Albert Swinestein

Pigmund Freud

"Sometimes a cigar is just a cigar."

The profundity of this statement alone would have assured the Austrian theorist recognition as one of the great analysts of the brain of pigs and the condition of swine in the modern world.

Not so sure-footed, Pigmund was also noted for *Freudian slips*. He was removed, probably prematurely, as a suckling and attributed the weakness in his hams and other leg muscles to this fact. Like many others who probed the depths of pigschology, he was prone to universalize his own repressed desires and foibles upon hogs in general.

"My investigations have shown conclusively that pigs are prone to respond to the stimuli of food and sex. They also respond to sex and food, but this is an indication that they've confused the priority of id versus ego," Pigmund explains.

"We are all a bit neurotic," he concludes, "Which, of course, is great for business."

Pigmund Freud

Section 3

Pigs and Sport

Road Hog

Some motorcyclists insist on hogging the center of the road. Road Hog here is fond of barreling "Swift-ly" down the highway, keeping his bike on the center line.

Little does he know that a little dog is coming in the opposite direction. Road Hog doesn't give an oink about the poor little dog.

He should!

The little dog is made of chrome and is on the hood of a giant Mack truck.

Road Hog

Show Us Your...

Unfortunately, not all porcine bikers are ladies and gentlemen. The couple here belong to the dreaded motorcycle gang, The Deviled Hams.

From the lakes of New Hampshire to the plains of South Dakota, The Deviled Hams assemble to create havoc at biker events. This hog and his sow are making sure they get the exposure that they so much crave.

We certainly do not condone such "boarish" behavior.

Show Us Your...

Pork Chopper

Pork Chopper has his special customized chopper. Any more chopped and it would be sausage!

His favorite taunt is, "When pigs fly!" And fly he does. In the tradition of Evil Pignievel he once attempted to jump twelve hog trailers.

Unfortunately, he ran out of air time at trailer number eleven.

They patched him up at The Jimmy Dean Hospital and Sausage Factory.

Pork Chopper

Hog Bless America

There is nothing quite as American as a big Harley Hog. A Hamaha just doesn't cut the mustard! Any pork worth his salt will have nothing to do with these ham fried rice rockets.

You gotta ride a hog. The bigger the better. And if you roast your hocks on the hot manifold, so much the better.

Roaring down the Interstate, flags flying in the wind, it's great to be free. Hog Bless America!

Hog Bless America

This Car's Got a Hami

NASCAR is becoming the most popular sport in America. Denny Hogfair here is typical of the great drivers who make the sport so popular.

The roar of the drivers, the smell of the crowd—this is truly twenty-first century American theatre. Where else can pigs spend entire weekends swilling beer and breathing foul exhaust, while being deafened by the noise?

Denny is backed up by one of the best pit crews in racing. When he pulls in for a pit stop, they are ready with a full pit barbecue. They can change baby back ribs, pull pork and slather on their secret sauce in less than fifteen seconds.

This Car's Got A Hami

Pigs Can Flyfish

You know the old expression, "When pigs can flyfish!" Well, they can.

Isaac Walt-ham here is an accomplished flyfisherman. A dry fly purist at that. From the chalk streams of England to the wild rivers of Patagonia, he has pitted his porcine piscatorial prowess with the most challenging of game fish. And Isaac has caught his fair share of hogs!

In these days of P. C. "catch and release," Isaac is an anomaly. He eats everything he catches. He calls it "catch and fillet." When asked why, he replies modestly, "Hey, I'm a pig."

Pigs Can Flyfish

Fenway Frank

Frank here knows everything about Fenway Park and The Sox.

Frank can tell you every Fenway fact from pole to pole (the Pesky pole to the Fisk pole). He can describe every game he's seen. And many a game he'd like to forget. When it comes to recalling games, Frank's a regular Hormel Allen.

As for statistics, Frank is a virtual piggy bank of information. From Sidepork (Cy) Young's ERA to Ted Willhams batting average, to Wade Hogg's good luck pieces, to the number of bricks in Porky Way...

If you were to call Fenway Frank an *idiot savant*, you'd be half right.

Fenway Frank

Ben HOGan

Ben was born a good ol' Texas hog. He began his golf career caddying as a wee piglet and went on to become one of the greatest golfers of all time.

He was known as "The Hogwk" because of his determination and iron will that intimidated opponents. On the course, he was taciturn to a tee. He might oink to an opponent at the start and give a soft squeal at the end. Otherwise he was silent.

In 1953, he incredibly won five of the six tournaments which he entered. A feat which is still known as the "HOGan Spam Slam."

Ben HOGan

Riding Piggyback

They're known as equestrihams, an elite group of pigs devoted to horseback riding. They can be found riding to the hounds or perhaps in a show ring. These are the top hogs of pigdom.

The old equestriham sport of Garbage Hunting has been much in the news of late.

There has been heavy protest from PETRE, People for the Ethical Treatment of REfuse.

It has even been banned in Great Britain. In this time-honored sport porcine riders chase hounds in search of garbage. Once the garbage is found, the hounds run it to cover.

Thinking such a grand sport is inhumane is, quite frankly, pure rubbish.

Riding Piggyback

Pigskin Pride

Every Sunday during the season, you can find him here. His little pig eyes glued to the HD TV. This guy's a New England Patriots fan, but he could just as well be a Pittsburgh Squealer fan or even a Washington Red Hog fan. Hail to Pig Skin Pride!

In bars and living rooms all across America, these fans gather to root and snort for their favorite teams, to swill their brewskis and munch on pickled pigs feet, (sometimes their own).

This stalwart fan always carries his lucky football with him. When asked why, he'll proudly tell you. "That's my Dad. He played in a Super Bowl."

Pigskin Pride

Hog Heaven

Somewhere in this favored land there's a Happy Hunting Ground right here on earth.

A place where the ponds and streams teem with hungry trout and salmon. A place where the fields and thickets abound with game. A place where the camaraderie is Arcadian.

And after the chase, a roaring hearth, a good cigar and warm cognac welcome one to the lodge.

So where is this Hog Heaven for hunters and fishermen? You know full well that they never divulge their secret spots.

Hog Heaven

Section 4

Pigs and Pop Culture

Sometimes You Feel Like a Sow, Sometimes You Don't

I am so tired. Up in the morning before dawn. Chasing the little ones away from TV and video games and trying to get a good breakfast into them. The old hog doesn't even bother to roll out of bed until they're off to school. He lays into his food like I've stuck swill in front of him, sticks his snout in a newspaper, and I'm lucky if I can get a grunt of acknowledgment before he's burning rubber out the door.

And he acts like he's the only one that brings home the bacon. Always complaining that the place looks like a pigsty—if it does, it's because he's such a slob and I can't keep up with cleaning up after him.

Of course, then I have to rush around and get off to work myself. We couldn't pay half the bills around here without my paycheck, not that he ever looks at the bills, except to squeal like he's been stuck every time he sees a charge show up from my hairdresser. "Pigtails," he snorts. "You'd think they were enameling them with gold instead of just tying them up with ribbons." Hah, what does he know about fashion!?!

At work I'm on my feet all day and I have to smile and act pleasant to everyone. I work in the Complaint Department, but do you think that ever entitles me to complain? Whine, whine, whine, that's all I hear, night and day.

Then I have to truck around the little ones, stop for groceries, wash dishes, vacuum, cook dinner, (thank the Lord for those new microwavable Hungry Ham frozen entrees), do laundry. His Majesty comes home just long enough to throw on a leather jacket, then jumps on his Hawg and is off to the races. He'll show up again when he's hungry and then collapse into an arm-chair and create a pile of empty beer cans and pork rind wrappers as he channel surfs and complains that Monday Night Football isn't on seven days a week.

I had dreams once. I felt young and beautiful. I could have had a career in Sowmetology. I believed in glamour and romance. Now all I have to look forward to is a night of listening to full volume snoring. Then I'll get up in the morning and start in again.

Sometimes You Feel Like a Sow,
Sometimes You Don't

Red Hat Sowciety

Welcome to the place where there is fun after the litter-bearing years for sows of all walks of life. We believe silliness is the comic relief of life and, since we are all in it together, we might as well join red-painted hooves and go for the gusto together. Underneath the frivolity, we share a bond of affection, forged by common life experiences and a genuine enthusiasm for wherever life takes us next.

While visiting a friend in West Pens several years ago, Suey Ellen impulsively bought a bright red fedora at a thrift shop, for no other reason than that it was cheap and, she thought, quite dashing. She decided that her birthday gift to her dear friend, Linda Piggety, would be a vintage red hat and a purple accessory. Linda got so much enjoyment out of the hat and the accessory that Suey Ellen gave the same gift to another friend, then another, then another.

Our main responsibility is to have fun! We see this group as an opportunity for those who have shouldered various responsibilities at home and in the community their whole lives, to say goodbye to burdensome responsibilities and obligations for a little while. This is the place to have fun, pig-out and enjoy yourself. The refrain of the popular Red Hat Sowciety theme song by Grunt Hamline puts it rather bluntly: "All my life, I've done for you. Now it's my turn to do for me." We've thrown all other rules over the fence and are working to build a dis-organization within which we can all connect and eventually take over the world!

Red Hat Sowciety

Once by thy Lips...
Forever on thy Hips

Discipline, discipline, discipline!

If that doesn't work, try diet, diet, diet!

Pills are another alternative, but see your doctor first.

Surgery is perhaps a little *too* drastic. Most of us would rather not get carved up, no matter how many years of med school the guy with the knife has had.

If all else fails, remember, your mother loves you and they say that there's someone in the world for everyone. We weren't all meant to look like Twiggy.

Once by thy Lips,
Forever on thy Hips

Enjoying a Swine Cooler

Take time out to relax and enjoy the finer side of life.

The gentle fizz of carbonated bubbles is soothing to the ears.... The fine cut glass and exquisite manners of the waiter remind us that we live, after all, in a gentile, cultivated sowciety.

But, of course, it is the art of conversation that can make an outing into an event. There are a few important rules to follow:

Have fun and don't be afraid to take every opportunity to flirt.

Use a Virginia accent if you want to appear sophisticated. If you're not from Virginia, just start every sentence with "Y'all..."

Always wink at a gentleham. If he's not really a gentleham, wink at him anyway and he'll think you're pretty high-class, not just another piece of meat.

Always be polite, especially when you're about to say something cruel.

"Y'all know Sue-ie. God bless her, but have you noticed the hair growing on her chin?"

"Y'all know how much I love my cousin Jezebel, but that outfit she wore last Friday made her look like a witch."

Enjoying a Swine Cooler

Santa Hog

The lists get longer every year. And the toys get more expensive. I've had to refurbish the sleigh and the elves want higher pay. This is getting to be a tough business.

I wish the parents would be a little more inventive with names. Last year I'll bet that half the young ones on my list were named Dakota and the other half were named Jennifer. Hard to keep things straight. No wonder the government wants to put chips in their ears from the day they pop out. Male. Born 031401. Stall 752. Pink with pink eyes.

No problem getting young piggies to learn vocabulary that involves "I want..." They're well on their way to becoming the world's ultimate consumers. It would be nice if they could improve their spelling, though. I get letters addressed to the North Pile, instead of the North Pole, and saying the latest Game Box would be swill, (read "swell"), but please include all the most vylet gayms, (i.e.—they like blood and guts).

I still clean up on milk and cookies, though—one of the big side benefits of the job. Trouble is, either my sides are getting bigger or those chimneys are shrinking.

Santa Hog

Rush Limboar

Rush: Listen, my friends, you are tuned to the-most-listened-to pig talk radio show in America.

All across the fruited plain, pigs are listening. Today, I'd like to ask you a question or two about your take on pork barrel legislation. Yep, it's happening right now at that big sty they call Capitol Hill. They're snorting and grunting and trying to get some fat back to their districts. Hold that thought!

Back after this...

SFX: (Theme music up and under)

ANNCR: Subscribe today to the Limboar Report. It's the report for pigs with only right wing hams. Phone 800-555-BOAR.

Rush: Friends, it's time to ask ourselves how we can rise above the Liberal porkers and oink, oink, oink, oink, oink, oink...

Rush Limboar

You've Got Mail

I love that special voice that sings from the speakers of my PC. "You've got mail!" it announces cheerily. Maybe it's another one of those side-splitting, off-color jokes from Uncle Hairy. Or maybe I'll find out that the eBay auction for the world's largest food trough has come down to the final minutes and I only need to add ten dollars to remain the highest bidder.

Cyber-World is great. So many things coming at you. Any information you want just a few clicks away from the old three-jointed hoof. Last night I put a ticker running across the top of my desktop: "Feed Corn: $4.50/bushel, Soy Beans: $3.30/bushel, et cetera, et cetera." It's comforting to see those commodities just keep on coming.

Of course, there's always someone trying to sell you something you don't really need. Hair removal systems, hair growing tonics, ointments for your snout, ointments for your ears, ointments for body parts there shouldn't be ointments for. Of course, I've put up the usual blockers to cut down the flow a bit, but these greasy slimeballs are more clever at finding ways to slide stuff under the door than the geeks are at shutting the loopholes.

So in order to see those pictures of Cousin Mary's brood at the latest family picnic or to hear a rip-snorter from my pen-pal in Iowa, I've got to sift through dozens of thinly disguised ads from herds of folk I hope I'll never have to meet. Spam. Spam. Spam. Don't they realize how upsetting this is to a pig.

Click and drag. Down it goes, into the trash can—the most heavily used icon on my screen.

You've Got Mail

Forrest Grunt

"Life is like a box of chocolates: you never know what you're going to get."

FORREST GRUNT (1994) is the story of an incredibly kind and gentle pig who is also what some might call "below average" in intelligence. It's true that he's not too smart, but he is very fortunate to have a mother and friends who love him dearly. Forrest, (played by Tom Shanks), is born and raised in rural Alabama. He grows up with his mother, who rents out stalls in the family barn to itinerant (and sometimes unruly) hogs.

Despite his lack of sophistication and the fact that he was raised far from any major cities, Forrest manages to become personally involved in many of the critical events that take place in recent American history. It should be no surprise that pigs were involved in the Vietnam war, the Watergate Scandal, the Civil Rights and anti-Vietnam war protest movements, and the computer revolution.

In a way, this movie is a look at a period of American history through the eyes of a creature who lacks swinecism, but simply accepts things as they are. Sometimes he accompanies his remarks with the truthful observation, "Stupid is as stupid does." Grunt is also incredibly lucky at every enterprise he attempts and in his relationships with others and is a "natural" at ping-pong, but this is nothing special for a pig.

Forrest Grunt

The Three Ham Slicers NYUK NYUK

One time vaudeville actors, the comedy trio acted in scores of Hoggywood two-reel short film productions, specializing in splapstick humor, runaway insults, and other typical boarish behavior. In one of these episodes, they are inept deliveryswine for a brewery. When they learn about a company golf tournament, they sneak onto the course to get some practice and a try at the hundred dollar prize. They quickly proceed to bother the other golfers and destroy the course. Forced to escape in their beer truck, more havoc ensues when the load of barrels are spilled out down a steep hill. Eight slaps, six conks to the head and two eye pokes (plus two blocked pokes).

Also the memorable line about the effect swilling too much beer can have on your form (swing): "Some foam, eh, kid?"

The Three Ham Slicers NYUK NYUK

The Hogfather

"My father made him an offer he couldn't refuse . . . [He] assured him, that either his brain or his signature would be on the contract."

Fear is still an important element in law and order in today's society and there are certain unsavory characters who are willing to use the rough methods they learned in the pigsty to earn a certain level of "respect." Marlon Grunter was so convincing in the role of Don Quarterham that it gave him the opportunity to show that he could avoid accepting a Hogscar with the best of them.

Even though most of Don Quarterham's enemies never came back, (except in jars or cans), the Hoggywood meat grinder had no trouble putting out THE HOGFATHER II, which brought back Mario Pigzo and co-starred Hogbert DeNiro. It made even more money than the first episode and really pigged out at the Hammy Awards.

The Hogfather

Section 5

Pigs and Parody

Male Chauvinist Pig

This chap's a real boar! Male Chauvinist Pig is a throwback to a different era. No wonder this pork jerky has had several cases of hamrassment brought against him.

Some of his female pickup lines are true classics.

"Heh, Babe, it's time for makin' bacon."

"Soooooooooooeeeeeeeeee. I'd like to smoke your butt."

Or his more creative, "Hey, Sow Baby, let me blow behind your ear. I bet I can make it into a silk purse."

What this lout needs is to read some Gloria Steinham.

Male Chauvinist Pig

Why You Never Feed Pigs Bubblegum

WASHINGTON—Fighter jets scrambled to the scene early Friday afternoon as a large number of unidentified objects suddenly appeared on radar screens heading directly toward the capital from the west. Major General "Pop" Chewinham says that the blips disappeared a few minutes later before positive identification could be made.

"A few of our pilots made visual contact and reported spotting large, slow-moving pink objects," Chewinham stated, "but the objects disappeared into thin air over a heavily-wooded Maryland hillside before the pilots could get closer and make more detailed observations."

The incident triggered a scarlet alert and Air Force One was briefly diverted as the President was returning from a campaign stop where he vigorously attacked "the pork-barrel politics of opportunists on Capitol Hill."

Why You Never Feed Pigs Bubblegum

Pork π

In human mythology and mathematics, pi, (π), is derived from the Greek symbol for "p" because of its relationship to perimeter.

But swine mathematicians have more correctly observed that pi stands for pig and is integrally related to all functions pertaining to a circle because pigs are always at the center of things.

As a number that cannot be written as a repeating decimal or a finite decimal (you can never get to the end of it) pi is irrational: it cannot be written as a fraction (the ratio of two integers). Pigs also enjoy being irrational and don't care to see themselves divided into fractions—or into sausage links either, for that matter.

Of course, pigs also enjoy pies of every description and have a saying every piglet knows:

Pi may remain constant
at 3.1415...,
but the bigger the pie,
the bigger the di [diameter],
And the more I like it.

Pork π

How Much Wood Would Pork Chop Chop if Pork Chop Could Chop Wood?

Pigs have been poorly represented in nursery rhymes. The exception being the classic couplet which every piglet knows:

> *This little piggy went to market.*
> *This little piggy stayed home.*

[Piglets having cloven hooves, so that is the full extent of the rhyme. Humans add a few extra lines to match the count of their toes.]

Less familiar is the lively limerick:

> *There was a young pig who chopped wood*
> *And chop wood he would when he could,*
>
>> *But the day came to be*
>> *When the axe chopped his knee*
>
> *Now the piggy's too chopped to chop wood.*

The reason for this blatant discrimination against pig rhymes can be laid squarely on the shoulders of Mother Goose herself. She has shamelessly used *Avis* nepotism in selecting characters for her rhymes. In some cases she has actually changed the names of pig characters. For example: "Orky Porky sat on a wall" or "To market, to market, to buy a fat sow."

*How much wood would PORK CHOP chop
if PORK CHOP could chop wood?*

Orkypay

Orkypay is a pig Latin Master. He's always been in love with that ancient and quite dead language.

At the drop of a fig leaf, he will quote from Julius Caesar. "All pigs from Gaul are divided into three parts. The first part is the Belgium ham..." Orkypay is equally adept at quoting from Cicero, a town not far from the Chicago meat packing plants.

Pity the generations of unfortunate piglets who had to conjugate pig Latin verbs under Orkypay's stern stare! He is particularly fond of the pluperfect subjunctive which we believe has something to do with wishing that Orkypay were butchered, cured and smoked.

Orkypay

Kosher Ham on Wry

Oink-vey! This one is *meshuganah*. My *Bubbe* would *plotz*, if she saw it. I refuse to write any more of this *treyf drek*.

(translation at bottom)

meshuganah -- crazy
Bubbe -- grandmother
plotz -- fall down dead right now [can be crude]
treyf -- not kosher and tends to go well with cocktail sauce
drek -- [is crude] ed.

Kosher Ham on Wry

Not With My Sweet Butt!

Ya'll stay away from my bodacious Virginia booty!

First, you ask to pickle my feet. Next, you want to cure my hocks. Then, you try to smoke my legs, after inviting me to some sort of picnic. Now, ya'll are fixin' to honey bake my butt. And it don't make no never mind if I'm attached to it or not.

Honey baked? Not with my Sweet Butt! My Southern hospitality has been worn thinner than a poor country preacher's frock coat. Why don't you go back up North and open up a can of Spam or whatever ya'll do up there?

Not With My Sweet Butt!

No Pigging Out—This Means You!

Too much of anything can be dangerous. Well, maybe there's no such thing as too much of **Pigs ina Poke**™, but it's still wise to take even this in small doses. If you really *must* have more, you can go to *http://www.pigsinapoke.com* and you'll see links to all kinds of wonderful **Pigs ina Poke**™ pigphenalia such as cards, T-shirts, ornaments, shadow boxes and framable quality prints. We keep adding to the list of artwork and reproductions, so check in periodically.

And soon there will be Collection #2, Collection #3 . . . . After suffering through some of our puns, you may have a good idea of your own you'd like to share with us, so please e-mail us at *dah@pigsinapoke.com*.

No Pigging Out — This Means You!

About the Authors and More about Pigs ina Poke™

Duane Hammond, aka D. A. Hammond, is a Buckingham Scholarship graduate from the Museum School of Fine Arts, Boston, Massachusetts (1964).

Immediately after graduation, until 1969, he worked as a graphic designer and art director for advertising agencies in New Hampshire and Boston.

In 1969 he started his own graphic design company , The Magnificent Art Machine, and in 1981 the name was changed to Hammond Design Associates, Inc. For thirty-nine years, Duane produced award-winning sales and marketing literature and advertising materials for many businesses. Some of his national and multi-national clients included EG&G, Inc., Data General, Bell & Howell, Sylvania and Compaq plus manufacturers, financial institutions and non-profit organizations.

He has won many awards for his design including two NH Graniteer Best of Show Awards, Hatch Awards, Boston and New York Art Directors Awards, Desi Awards and over thirty-five more from other recognized trade groups. He has also had his work published in such prestigious magazines as PRINT and CA.

Now semi-retired, Duane spends his time painting pastels and watercolors. He has won several awards for his work and his paintings are on exhibit and for sale throughout New Hampshire in many galleries.

Duane is a member of the New Hampshire Artists Association, Manchester Art Association, Sharon Art Center, and the Durham Art Association.

His painting style includes impressionism and realism. Subjects range from seascapes, landscapes and cityscapes to wildlife and a series of whimsical, satirical pigs.

The three pigs unmasked: Larry, Brad, and Duane.

Lawrence K. DeLamarter is the owner of DeLamarter Advertising Services, Inc. in Concord, Massachusetts. He is on the faculty at

Boston University as a lecturer in the Communications department, teaching primarily Advertising. He received his B.A. from the University of Colorado; M.A., Universidad de las Americas (Mexico). He is an avid golfer, (when he plays golf), fisherman, hunter and outdoorsman.

Bradley Marion is the publisher of Beech River Books and co-editor (with Fred Moe) of *Color Wheel*, a journal celebrating literary and fine arts in a metaphysical world. He received his B.A. from Belknap College, Center Harbor, N.H. and M.Ed. from Plymouth State University in Plymouth, N.H. He is the author of two books of poetry and teaches in the field of Special Education with young adolescents. His wife, Dawn, is a oil painter and illustrator and his son, Ethan, is a graphic artist.

Pigs ina Poke™ is a wonderful collection of satirical and whimsical pigs in artwork created since 2003 by D. A. Hammond. Mr. Hammond and his art have been featured on television on NEW HAMPSHIRE CHRONICLES, in *Decor* magazine, and in numerous local and regional publications and newspapers. You can go on-line to *http://www.pigsinapoke.com* and you'll see links to all kinds of wonderful **Pigs ina Poke**™ pigphenalia such as cards, T-shirts, ornaments, shadow boxes and framable quality prints. We keep adding to the list of artwork and reproductions, so check in periodically.

And soon there will be Collection #2, Collection #3 . . . . After suffering through some of our puns, you may have a good idea of your own you'd like to share with us, so please e-mail us at *dah@pigsinapoke.com*.

The End, Butt...

Look for Collection #2, (Coming Soon!)